1. Introduction

In order to better understand the features and consumer protections currently provided by prepaid products, the Bureau conducted a study (the Study) of publicly available account agreements for prepaid products. The prepaid products included in the Study all appeared to meet the proposed definition of the term prepaid account in its proposed rule governing prepaid accounts under the Electronic Fund Transfer Act (Regulation E) and the Truth in Lending Act (Regulation Z), published concurrently herewith. Specifically, the Bureau sought to determine current industry practices in a number of areas to inform the Bureau's understanding of the potential benefits and costs of extending various Regulation E provisions to prepaid accounts. In conducting the Study, Bureau staff examined certain key provisions in the account agreements of prepaid cards and other similar prepaid programs currently available to consumers and compared those terms against the protections that would be required by the proposal.

The Study covers 325 account agreements for prepaid programs that, Bureau staff believes, could be subject to the definition of prepaid account in the Bureau's proposed rule.[1] This Study examines key provisions regarding error resolution protections (including provisional credit); limited liability protections; access to account information; overdraft services and negative balance fees; Federal Deposit Insurance Corporation (FDIC) or National Credit Union Share Insurance Fund (NCUSIF) pass-through deposit or share insurance; and general disclosure of fee information. The proposed rule explains in detail the issues related to these various provisions.

The Bureau notes that many of the provisions in its proposed rule are similar to existing requirements for certain types of prepaid products. Regulation E currently applies to payroll

---

[1] The Bureau does not intend for a prepaid account agreement's inclusion in or exclusion from the Study to be a determination as to whether the proposed rule would or would not apply to that prepaid program.

card accounts and cards used for the distribution of certain government benefits.[2] In addition, an interim final rule issued in 2010 by the Department of the Treasury's Financial Management Service, now part of Treasury's Bureau of the Fiscal Service, requires all prepaid cards receiving Federal payments (such as social security benefits, Federal tax refunds, or wages from the Federal government) to satisfy several conditions, including that the card issuer must comply with all of the requirements of, and provide the cardholder with all of the consumer protections that apply to, a payroll card account under Regulation E (the FMS Rule).[3]

A spreadsheet containing the text of relevant provisions from each account agreement and Bureau staff's analysis thereof, as described below, is attached hereto as Attachment A.[4]

The Bureau cautions that the analysis in this Study is, in many ways, subjective and thus is not an assessment of any legal issue including whether a prepaid program actually complies with or is in violation of Regulation E's existing provisions governing payroll card accounts or cards used for the distribution of certain government benefits, the FMS Rule, or the Bureau's proposed rule for prepaid accounts.

---

[2] *See* 12 CFR 1005.18 and 1005.15.

[3] *See* 31 CFR 210.5(b)(5).

[4] http://files.consumerfinance.gov/f/201411_cfpb_attachment-a-to-study-prepaid-account-agreements.xls.

2. Prepaid account agreements included in the Study

2.1 Identification of prepaid account agreements for inclusion in the Study

To determine the universe of prepaid account agreements to include in the Study, Bureau staff began by compiling account agreements for general purpose reloadable (GPR) prepaid card programs listed on the Visa, MasterCard, and NerdWallet websites advertising such cards and those examined in various other studies of prepaid card terms.[5] Staff obtained these account agreements online, and excluded prepaid programs for which agreements were unavailable as well as agreements for programs that staff believed had been discontinued.

Next, Bureau staff also searched for account agreements from prepaid programs belonging to entities involved in the prepaid marketplace of which staff was aware through the Bureau's general market monitoring efforts. Staff conducted additional research to identify issuers and program managers for prepaid products and to locate account agreements for programs offered by such entities, including a review of products offered by entities that had submitted comment letters in response to the Bureau's May 2012 Advance Notice of Proposed Rulemaking on GPR cards,[6] entities registered as providers of prepaid access (a type of money services business) with the Financial Crimes Enforcement Network (FinCEN),[7] and entities that had commented on

---

[5] *See generally* CFPB, *Arbitration Study Preliminary Results, Section 1028(a) Study Results to Date,* at 134-35 (Dec. 12, 2013), *available at* http://files.consumerfinance.gov/f/201312_cfpb_arbitration-study-preliminary-results.pdf.

[6] 77 FR 30923 (May 24, 2012). *See* http://www.regulations.gov/#!docketDetail;D=CFPB-2012-0019.

[7] *See* http://www.fincen.gov/financial_institutions/msb/msbstateselector.html.

FinCEN's prepaid access proposal in 2010.[8] Finally, staff engaged in additional internet research to identify other prepaid account agreements for inclusion in the Study.

The Study includes account agreements for GPR card programs (including GPR cards marketed for specific purposes, such as travel or receipt of tax refunds, or for specific users, such as teenagers or students), as well as payroll cards, cards used for the distribution of certain government benefits, and similar card programs.[9] Agreements for prepaid programs specifically usable for person-to-person (P2P) transfers that appear to be encompassed in the Bureau's proposed definition of prepaid account are also included. The Study does not include gift, incentive and rebate card programs; health spending account, flexible spending account, and similar card programs; or needs-tested State or local electronic benefit transfer (EBT) card programs, as such products are outside the scope of the Bureau's proposed prepaid accounts rulemaking.

Bureau staff collected prepaid account agreements between August 2013 and September 2014. Agreements collected appeared to be current at the time they were obtained and reviewed, but it is possible that outdated versions of some agreements were located online. Even if current at the time of collection, such agreements may not, however, all be current now. If staff became aware that a particular prepaid program was no longer operational, the agreement for that program was removed from the Study. However, it is possible that not all programs for which agreements were included in the Study are operational now.

In the Study, Bureau staff used only prepaid account agreements that were publicly available online. Where a prepaid account agreement did not include fee information, staff searched for a separate document containing fee information. In limited instances, where a prepaid account agreement did not appear to address certain key provisions, staff also used other publicly available materials such as FAQs related to that prepaid program. However, staff did not, as a general matter, review prepaid programs' websites, marketing materials, or other documents for additional information.

---

[8] *See* http://www.regulations.gov/#!docketDetail;D=FINCEN-2009-0007.

[9] As noted above, payroll card accounts and cards used for the distribution of certain government benefits are currently subject to Regulation E. *See* 12 CFR 1005.18 and 1005.15. The government benefit cards included in this Study are limited to those that Bureau staff believes are currently covered by Regulation E.

While Bureau staff collected a large number of agreements, the Bureau cautions that this collection is neither comprehensive nor complete. As discussed above, staff only included programs whose agreements were readily available online. In addition, there does not currently exist any comprehensive listing of all prepaid issuers, program managers, or programs that the Bureau could use to identify prepaid programs for inclusion in the Study.

2.2 Breakdown of prepaid account agreements reviewed in the Study

The Study covers 325 prepaid account agreements. Where what appears to be a single prepaid program has more than one account agreement, such as for different fee plans or for cards issued by different banks, all agreements identified by Bureau staff were included in the Study. Thus, while the Study includes 325 prepaid account agreements, it likely reflects fewer than 325 distinct prepaid programs.[10]

The Bureau notes that in the various statistics provided throughout the Study, equal weight is given to each agreement reviewed. These percentages do not reflect individual programs' or providers' market shares, although the Bureau attempts to correct for that bias somewhat by providing analysis specifically for agreements that belong to program managers (including issuers that manage their own programs) in the GPR card marketplace identified by one source as representing a combined market share (as of late 2012) of 81 percent based on load volume and 85 percent on number of active cards.[11]

---

[10] *See* Attachment A at column A for program name.

[11] *See* Aite Group LLC, The Contenders: Prepaid Debit and Payroll Cards Reach Ubiquity, at 17 and 23 (Nov. 2012).

A breakdown of the types of programs for which agreements are included in the Study, as identified by Bureau staff, is set forth in Table 1.[12]

TABLE 1:   BREAKDOWN OF PROGRAM TYPES INCLUDED IN THE STUDY

Type of prepaid program	Number of agreements reviewed	Percentage of total agreements reviewed
GPR cards[13]	207	63.69%
Payroll cards[14]	25	7.69%
Government benefit cards[15]	65	20.00%
All other programs[16]	28	8.62%
Total	**325**	

---

[12] *See* Attachment A at column B for program type and column C for program subtype, where applicable.

[13] This includes 5 GPR cards identified as marketed towards students, 6 for distribution of tax refunds, 6 for teenagers, and 7 for travel.

[14] As noted above, the Study includes payroll cards that are currently subject to Regulation E through existing § 1005.18.

[15] As noted above, the Study includes government benefit cards that are currently subject to Regulation E through existing § 1005.15. The Study is not intended to include any needs-tested State or local EBT card programs.

[16] This includes 1 emergency relief card, 1 non-reloadable non-gift card, 1 government tax refund card, 1 student refund card, 2 insurance cards, 3 student financial aid disbursement cards, 5 prison release cards, 7 P2P programs, and 7 cards similarly used for other specific purposes.

The agreements reviewed cover approximately 78 distinct issuing institutions and 141 distinct program managers.[17] The breakdown of issuers and program managers based on the type of program is set forth in Table 2.

TABLE 2:   NUMBER OF ISSUERS AND PROGRAM MANAGERS REPRESENTED (BY PROGRAM TYPE)

Type of prepaid program	Number of issuers	Number of program managers
GPR cards	62	118
Payroll cards	19	20
Government benefit cards	5	4
All other programs	16	16
Totals (all agreements)[18]	**78**	**141**

---

[17] *See* Attachment A at column D for program manager name and column E for issuer name. If it appeared to Bureau staff that an issuer also acts as program manager for a particular program, the issuer's name is included in both columns. Column E contains the relevant payment network's name.

The numbers given for program managers include issuers in situations where the issuer also functions as program manager for the program in question. While the issuers identified in the Study are largely banks and credit unions, the numbers given for issuers also include several non-banks where Bureau staff was unable to identify a separate bank or credit union issuer for the program in question. If these overlaps are removed, the Study covers approximately 173 unique entities.

[18] The Bureau notes that the total number of issuers and program managers reflected here across these four program types is greater than the totals across all agreements of 78 and 141, respectively, because some issuers and program managers are involved in more than one type of prepaid program.

3. Analysis of key provisions in prepaid account agreements

As noted above, the Study examined key provisions regarding error resolution protections (including provisional credit); limited liability protections; access to account information; overdraft and treatment of negative balances and declined transaction fees; FDIC or NCUSIF pass-through deposit or share insurance; and general disclosure of fees. Bureau staff's methodology, key assumptions, observations, and findings with respect to each of these categories are discussed below.

In addition, as noted above, the Bureau cautions that the analysis in this Study is, in many ways, subjective and thus is not an assessment of any legal issue including whether a prepaid program actually complies with or is in violation of Regulation E's existing provisions governing payroll card accounts or cards used for the distribution of certain government benefits, the FMS Rule, or the Bureau's proposed rules for prepaid accounts.

3.1 Error resolution protections (including provisional credit)

As described in more detail in the Supplementary Information to the Bureau's proposed rule, Regulation E requires that a covered financial institution promptly investigate an electronic fund transfer reported by a consumer as unauthorized, determine whether an error occurred, and correct any such errors. If the financial institution is unable to complete the investigation within ten business days,[19] its investigation may take up to 45 days[20] if it provisionally credits the amount of the alleged error back to the consumer's account within ten business days of receiving the error notice.[21]

Bureau staff examined relevant language in prepaid account agreements addressing error resolution in order to assess whether each program provided by contract the same error resolution protections that Regulation E requires for accounts to which it applies. Agreements were divided into four categories: (1) full error resolution with provisional credit available for all consumers where the error could not be resolved within a defined period of time; (2) error resolution with limitations on provisional credit (for example, when provisional credit is only provided for accounts that receive Federal payments or payroll direct deposits); (3) error resolution but no provisional credit; and (4) no error resolution.[22]

Bureau staff focused on the key elements of error resolution and provisional credit. Staff observed that a number of agreements deviated from Regulation E as to their timing requirements (for example, with respect to the time periods given for a consumer to report an error, or for the financial institution to review and resolve an error claim). For example, some agreements stated a more limited time period during which a consumer could assert errors, such as 60 or 90 days from the date of the alleged error or the date the alleged error appeared on the consumer's transaction history, rather than 60 days from the date the consumer accessed his electronic history or requested a written history on which the alleged error first appeared. Because of the frequency with which variations in the timing requirements appeared, and because the Bureau does not believe it would be burdensome for prepaid providers to modify the

---

[19] The financial institution has 20 days (instead of 10) if the claimed unauthorized electronic fund transfer occurred within 30 days after the first deposit to the account was made. *See* § 1005.11(c)(3)(i). Provisional credit is not required if the financial institution requires but does not receive written confirmation within 10 business days of an oral notice by the consumer. *See* § 1005.11(c)(2)(i)(A).

[20] The financial institution has 90 days (instead of 45) if the claimed unauthorized electronic fund transfer was not initiated in a state, resulted from a point-of-sale debit card transaction, or occurred within 30 days after the first deposit to the account was made. *See* § 1005.11(c)(3)(ii).

[21] Regulation E also prescribes time frames for the consumer to report a suspected error, and for the financial institution to notify the consumer of the investigation's results, and to correct the error if one occurred. *See* § 1005.11.

[22] *See* Attachment A at column G for the text of each agreement's error resolution provisions. *See* columns H through K for Bureau staff's analysis of those provisions.

timing provisions of their error resolution procedures, Bureau staff did not take into account these timing variations in assessing agreements' error resolution provisions.

If an agreement did not mention provisional credit or made only a vague reference to some form of "credit" being provided, staff presumed that the program would not provide provisional credit. A determination of "no error resolution" was made where the account agreement either stated that the program did not provide any error resolution protection or was silent with respect to error resolution protections.

Table 3 summarizes Bureau staff's findings regarding error resolution and provisional credit protections across all 325 prepaid account agreements reviewed; for agreements broken down by GPR cards, payroll cards, government benefit cards, and all other programs; and for GPR card agreements that belong to program managers (including issuers that manage their own programs) in the GPR card marketplace identified by one source as representing a combined market share (as of late 2012) of 81 percent based on load volume (5 entities) and 85 percent on number of active cards (11 entities).[23]

TABLE 3: ERROR RESOLUTION AND PROVISIONAL CREDIT FINDINGS

Scope of review	Full error resolution with provisional credit		Error resolution with limitations on provisional credit		Error resolution but no provisional credit		No error resolution	
All agreements	**253**	**77.85%**	**40**	**12.31%**	**30**	**9.23%**	**2**	**0.62%**
GPR cards	141	68.12%	40	19.32%	25	12.08%	1	0.48%
Payroll cards	25	100%	0	--	0	--	0	--
Government benefit cards	65	100%	0	--	0	--	0	--
All other programs	22	78.57%	0	--	5	17.86%	1	3.57%
GPR only: 5 largest program managers by load volume	17	77.27%	3	13.64%	2	9.09%	0	--
GPR only: 11 largest program managers by number of active cards	32	80.0%	6	15.0%	2	5.0%	0	--

---

[23] *See* Aite Group LLC, *The Contenders: Prepaid Debit and Payroll Cards Reach Ubiquity,* at 17 and 23 (Nov. 2012). The Bureau notes that the data provided here and elsewhere throughout the Study for agreements belonging to these top 5 (by load volume) and top 11 (by number of active cards) program managers weight the findings equally across all included programs; findings are not weighted by relative market share.

3.2 Limited liability protections

As described in more detail in the Supplementary Information to the Bureau's proposed rule, Regulation E provides that a consumer may be held liable for an unauthorized electronic fund transfer resulting from the loss or theft of an access device only if the financial institution has provided certain required disclosures and other conditions are met.[24] If the consumer provides timely notice to the financial institution within two business days of learning of the loss or theft of the access device, the consumer's liability is the lesser of $50 or the amount of unauthorized transfers made before giving notice.[25] If timely notice is not given, the consumer's liability is the lesser of $500 or the sum of (1) the lesser of $50 or the amount of unauthorized transfers occurring within two business days of learning of the loss/theft and (2) the amount of unauthorized transfers that occur after two business days but before notice is given to the financial institution.[26] In addition, a consumer must report an unauthorized electronic fund transfer that appears on a periodic statement within 60 days of the financial institution's transmittal of the statement in order to avoid liability for subsequent transfers.[27] The Bureau notes that the payment card network associations each have their own rules providing for zero cardholder liability for certain unauthorized transactions that occur on cards bearing the network's brand.

Bureau staff examined prepaid account agreements' language addressing limitations on consumers' liability for unauthorized transactions to assess whether each program provided by contract the same limited liability protections that Regulation E requires for accounts to which it applies. Agreements were divided into three categories: (1) liability limitations consistent with

---

[24] The required disclosures for this purpose include a summary of the consumer's liability under § 1005.6, or under state law or other applicable law or agreement, for unauthorized electronic fund transfers; the telephone number and address of the person or office to be notified when the consumer believes an unauthorized transfer has been or may be made; and the financial institution's business days. *See* §§ 1005.6(a), 1005.7(b)(1) through (3).

[25] *See* § 1005.6(b)(1).

[26] *See* § 1005.6(b)(2).

[27] *See* § 1005.6(b)(3).

Regulation E (or better); (2) some liability limitations but less than what is provided for by Regulation E; and (3) no limited liability protections.[28]

Bureau staff found that some agreements were unclear as to whether or to what extent consumers' liability for unauthorized transactions would be limited. A designation of "no limited liability" was used where the account agreement either stated that the program did not limit consumers' liability for unauthorized transactions or was silent with respect to liability limitations.

---

[28] *See* Attachment A at column L for the text of each agreement's limited liability provisions. *See* columns M through O for Bureau staff's analysis of those provisions.

Table 4 summarizes Bureau staff's findings regarding limited liability protections across all 325 account agreements reviewed; for agreements broken down by GPR cards, payroll cards, government benefit cards, and all other programs; and for GPR card agreements that belong to program managers (including issuers that manage their own programs) in the GPR card marketplace identified by one source as representing a combined market share (as of late 2012) of 81 percent based on load volume (5 entities) and 85 percent on number of active cards (11 entities).

TABLE 4: LIMITED LIABILITY FINDINGS

Scope of review	Full limited liability		Partial limited liability		No limited liability	
All agreements	**289**	**88.92%**	**27**	**8.31%**	**9**	**2.77%**
GPR cards	181	87.44%	22	10.63%	4	1.93%
Payroll cards	25	100%	0	--	0	--
Government benefit cards	65	100%	0	--	0	--
All other programs	18	64.28%	5	17.86%	5	17.86%
GPR only: 5 largest program managers by load volume	22	100%	0	--	0	--
GPR only: 11 largest program managers by number of active cards	40	100%	0	--	0	--

During the course of this portion of the review, Bureau staff also noted that a majority of agreements specifically mentioned the relevant card network's "zero liability" policy in addition to the agreement's other limited liability provisions.

Access to account information

With respect to consumers' access to account information, Bureau staff attempted to determine the following for each agreement: (1) whether the program provides electronic access to account history; (2) the time frame for which account information is available; (3) whether an electronic periodic statement is available; (4) whether consumers can request that paper periodic statements and/or histories of account transactions be mailed to them; and (5) if a paper statement or history can be requested, what the associated cost would be (if any).[29] Tables 5 through 10 summarize staff's findings for each of these five items in turn, across all 325 account agreements reviewed; for agreements broken down by GPR cards, payroll cards, government benefit cards, and all other programs; and for GPR card programs that belong to program managers (including issuers that manage their own programs) in the GPR card marketplace identified by one source as representing a combined market share (as of late 2012) of 81 percent based on load volume (5 entities) and 85 percent on number of active cards (11 entities).

---

[29] *See* Attachment A at column P for the text of each agreement's provisions regarding access to account information. *See* columns Q through U for Bureau staff's analysis of those provisions, as described in more detail below.

Table 5 summarizes Bureau staff's findings regarding electronic access to account history information. Staff was either able to confirm based on the agreement that electronic access to account information was available or the agreement was unclear as to whether such access was available. Staff found no agreements that specifically stated electronic access was not available.[30]

TABLE 5: ACCESS TO ACCOUNT INFORMATION (ELECTRONIC ACCESS TO ACCOUNT HISTORY) FINDINGS

Scope of review	Provides electronic access to account information		Unclear as to whether electronic access to account information is provided	
All agreements	**318**	**97.85%**	**7**	**2.15%**
GPR cards	205	99.03%	2	0.97%
Payroll cards	25	100%	0	--
Government benefit cards	65	100%	0	--
All other programs	23	82.14%	5	17.86%
GPR only: 5 largest program managers by load volume	22	100%	0	--
GPR only: 11 largest program managers by number of active cards	40	100%	0	--

---

[30] *See* Attachment A at column Q. Each agreement was designated as either Y (Yes) or Unclear.

Table 6 summarizes Bureau staff's findings regarding the time frames for which account information is available. Staff found that for agreements that list a specific time frame for which account information is available (whether electronically or in writing), the time frame ranges from 60 days to 2 years. Some agreements stated (or implied) that there is no limit on the length of time for which account information is available. For some agreements, staff was unable to determine the program's time frame.[31] Where an agreement lists different times frames for written and electronic account information, staff used the longer time frame for this analysis.[32]

TABLE 6:   ACCESS TO ACCOUNT INFORMATION (TIME FRAME) FINDINGS

Scope of review	60 days		90 days to 1 year		2 years		Unlimited		Unclear	
All agreements	215	66.15%	9	2.78%	7	2.16%	8	2.46%	86	26.46%
GPR cards	132	63.77%	7	3.38%	6	2.90%	8	3.86%	54	26.09%
Payroll cards	13	52.0%	2	8.0%	1	4.0%	0	--	9	36.0%
Government benefit cards	65	100%	0	--	0	--	0	--	0	--
All other programs	5	17.86%	0	--	0	--	0	--	23	82.14%
GPR only: 5 largest program managers by load volume	21	95.45%	0	--	0	--	0	--	1	4.55%
GPR only: 11 largest program managers by number of active cards	34	85.0%	0	--	4	10.0%	0	--	2	5.0%

---

[31] *See* Attachment A at column R. Each agreement was designated as either 60 days, 90 days, 120 days, 1 year, 2 years, Unlimited, or Unclear. For purposes of Table 6, the agreements designated as 90 days, 120 days or 1 year were combined.

[32] Based on the Bureau's outreach to industry in connection with the proposed rule, the Bureau is aware that many prepaid programs provide access to account information for much longer time frames than what is listed in their account agreements. Nevertheless, for purposes of the Study, staff assumed that a particular program's practice matched the stated terms in its agreement.

Table 7 summarizes Bureau staff's findings regarding the availability of electronic periodic statements. Staff found that some agreements specifically state that electronic periodic statements (rather than just electronic access to account history) are available.[33] Staff did not note any agreements that specifically state an electronic statement would not be provided. If an agreement does not mention electronic periodic statements, staff presumed such statements were not available.[34]

TABLE 7: ACCESS TO ACCOUNT INFORMATION (ELECTRONIC PERIODIC STATEMENTS) FINDINGS

Scope of review	Electronic periodic statements available		No electronic periodic statements	
All agreements	187	57.54%	138	42.46%
GPR cards	89	43.0%	118	57.0%
Payroll cards	20	80.0%	5	20.0%
Government benefit cards	62	95.38%	3	4.62%
All other programs	16	57.14%	12	42.86%
GPR only: 5 largest program managers by load volume	12	54.55%	10	45.45%
GPR only: 11 largest program managers by number of active cards	18	45.0%	22	55.0%

---

[33] Under Regulation E currently, financial institutions offering payroll card accounts either must provide periodic statements or must follow the periodic statement alternative which requires access to account balance information by phone, at least 60 days of electronic account history, and at least 60 days of written account history upon request. *See* 12 CFR 1005.18(b).

[34] *See* Attachment A at column S. Each agreement was designated as either Y (Yes) or N (No).

Table 8 summarizes Bureau staff's findings as to whether consumers can request that paper statements and/or paper account histories be mailed to them. If an agreement did not mention paper periodic statements or account histories, staff presumed such statements/histories were not available.[35]

TABLE 8: ACCESS TO ACCOUNT INFORMATION (PAPER STATEMENTS/ACCOUNT HISTORIES) FINDINGS

Scope of review	Paper statements/ account histories available		No paper statements/ account histories	
All agreements	290	89.23%	35	10.77%
GPR cards	183	88.41%	24	11.59%
Payroll cards	24	96.0%	1	4.0%
Government benefit cards	65	100%	0	--
All other programs	18	64.29%	10	35.71%
GPR only: 5 largest program managers by load volume	22	100%	0	--
GPR only: 11 largest program managers by number of active cards	39	97.50%	1	2.50%

The Bureau notes that if a prepaid program provides periodic statements and obtains E-Sign consent from all consumers to deliver those statements electronically,[36] the agreement would likely be designated as no paper statements/ account histories in Table 8.

Table 9 summarizes Bureau staff's findings as to whether, if a paper statement or paper account history could be requested, what the associated cost would be (if any).[37] This analysis excludes agreements that were designated in Table 8 as not providing paper periodic statements or paper account histories.[38] Where an agreement lists more than one fee amount for receiving a paper

---

[35] *See* Attachment A at column T. Each agreement was designated as either Y (Yes) or N (No).

[36] Currently, Regulation E permits disclosures to be provided in electronic form, subject to compliance with consumer consent and other applicable provisions of the Electronic Signatures in Global and National Commerce Act (E-Sign Act) (15 U.S.C. 7001, *et seq.*). *See* § 1005.4(a)(1).

statement and/or paper account history, staff used the higher fee (except in instances where the higher fee was only assessed for duplicated mailings).

TABLE 9: ACCESS TO ACCOUNT INFORMATION (COST OF PAPER STATEMENTS/ACCOUNT HISTORIES) FINDINGS

Scope of review	Free ($0)		Fee ($ listed)		Fee ($ not listed)		No fee information	
All agreements	94	32.41%	136	46.90%	25	8.62%	35	12.07%
GPR cards	51	27.87%	116	63.39%	10	5.46%	6	3.28%
Payroll cards	4	16.67%	13	54.17%	5	20.83%	2	8.33%
Government benefit cards	36	55.38%	2	3.08%	0	--	27	41.54%
All other programs	3	16.67%	5	27.78%	10	55.56%	0	--
GPR only: 5 largest program managers by load volume	9	40.91%	13	59.09%	0	--	0	--
GPR only: 11 largest program managers by number of active cards	20	51.28%	19	48.72%	0	--	0	--

Bureau staff encountered a number of challenges in the analysis of agreements for the information reflected in Table 9. For example, some agreements stated that no fee would be charged for paper statements or account histories but then listed a fee elsewhere in the

---

[37] *See* Attachment A at column U. If, based on the agreement, it did not appear that a program provides paper statements and/or paper account histories (designated as N in column T and reflected in the columns on the right in Table 8), the agreement was designated in column U as NA (not applicable). If an agreement specified a fee amount, the agreement was designated with that amount. If an agreement stated that paper statements and/or paper account histories would be provided for free, or otherwise suggested that a fee would not be charged, the agreement was designated as $0.

If it appeared from the text of an agreement that a fee may or will be charged, but staff was unable to locate fee information generally for that program, the agreement was designated as Fee. If the text of an agreement did not address whether or not a fee would be charged for a paper statement and/or paper account history, and Bureau staff was unable to locate fee information generally for the program, the agreement was designated here as No fee info. Remaining agreements for which Bureau staff was unable to make a determination were designated as Unclear.

[38] Those agreements are reflected in the "No paper statement/account history" column in Table 8.

agreement. Other agreements stated that a fee may or will be charged for paper statements or account histories but did specify the amount of that fee anywhere else in the document. In addition, as discussed further below, staff was unable to find fee information for a number of programs.[39]

Table 10 summarizes Bureau staff's more specific findings regarding fees charged for paper statements and/or paper account histories, including the mean (average), median, and range of fees charged (where a specific non-zero fee was listed in the agreement).[40] For agreements that specified the fee charged for providing paper statements and/or paper account histories, staff found that the amount of the fee varied widely across all programs (ranging from $0.75 to $10).

TABLE 10: ACCESS TO ACCOUNT INFORMATION (COST OF PAPER STATEMENTS/ACCOUNT HISTORIES – MEAN, MEDIAN, AND RANGE OF SPECIFIED FEES CHARGED) FINDINGS

Scope of review	Number and percent of agreements charging a specified fee[41]		Mean (Average)	Median	Range
All agreements	**136**	**46.90%**	**$ 3.54**	**$ 2.98**	**$ 0.75 - $ 10.00**
GPR cards	116	63.39%	$ 3.54	$ 3.00	$ 0.99 - $ 10.00
Payroll cards	13	54.17%	$ 2.92	$ 2.50	$ 1.00 - $ 5.00
Government benefit cards	2	3.08%	$ 1.13	$ 1.13	$ 0.75 - $ 1.50
All other programs	5	27.78%	$ 6.30	$ 5.00	$ 2.50 - $ 10.00
GPR only: 5 largest program managers by load volume	13	59.09%	$ 4.27	$ 5.95	$ 1.00 - $ 5.95
GPR only: 11 largest program managers by number of active cards	19	48.72%	$ 3.86	$ 3.00	$ 1.00 - $ 5.95

---

[39] Staff's treatment of these issues is described in footnote 37 above.

[40] Table 10 covers all agreements that specify a non-zero fee amount.

[41] This column in Table 10 corresponds with the "Fee ($ listed)" column in Table 9 and is repeated here for reference.

3.4 Overdraft services and negative balance fees

Bureau staff attempted to determine the following for each account agreement: (1) whether the program offers a formal opt-in overdraft service;[42] and (2) whether the program charges any fees related to negative balances, including overdraft fees, negative balance fees, shortage fees and insufficient funds fees (and if so, the amount of such fees).[43] Tables 11 and 12 below summarize staff's findings for each of these items in turn, across all 325 account agreements reviewed; for agreements broken down by GPR cards, payroll cards, government benefit cards, and all other programs; and for GPR card agreements that belong to program managers (including issuers that manage their own programs) in the GPR card marketplace identified by one source as representing a combined market share (as of late 2012) of 81 percent based on load volume (5 entities) and 85 percent on number of active cards (11 entities).

Bureau staff did not note any prepaid account agreements that appear to offer any formal credit features other than those identified as offering an opt-in overdraft service, as reflected in Table 11.

---

[42] *See* 12 CFR 1005.17.

[43] *See* Attachment A at column V for the text of each agreement's provisions regarding overdrafts, negative balance fees and general treatment of spending in excess of account balance. *See* columns W and X for Bureau staff's analysis of those provisions, as described in more detail below.

Table 11 summarizes Bureau staff's findings regarding agreements indicating that the program offers a formal opt-in overdraft service.[44] Staff assumed that, where an agreement did not address overdraft services, no such services were available.

TABLE 11: OVERDRAFT SERVICES FINDINGS

Scope of review	No overdraft service		"Purchase cushion" only		Overdraft service[45]	
All agreements	**314**	**96.62%**	**4**	**1.23%**	**7**	**2.15%**
GPR cards	198	95.65%	4	1.93%	5	2.42%
Payroll cards	25	100%	0	--	0	--
Government benefit cards	63	96.92%	0	--	2	3.08%
All other programs	28	100%	0	--	0	--
GPR only: 5 largest program managers by load volume	17	77.27%	2	9.09%	3	13.64%
GPR only: 11 largest program managers by number of active cards	35	87.50%	2	5.0%	3	7.50%

---

[44] *See* Attachment A at column W. Each agreement was designated as either Y (Yes), N (No), or Purchase cushion. The agreements designated as "purchase cushion" allow for consumers to overspend by a small amount but do not appear to require consumer opt-in and do not state a fee for that service.

[45] The Bureau notes that it is possible that some of the programs reflected here no longer offer overdraft services but the agreements for those programs available online have not been correspondingly updated.

Table 12 summarizes Bureau staff's findings regarding agreements for programs that might charge overdraft, negative balance, shortage, insufficient fund or similar fees.[46] Those agreements designated in Table 11 as offering formal opt-in overdraft services are included in Table 12 as charging fees for negative balances, as are others that typically state that a cardholder is not permitted to conduct transactions in excess of the card balance, but that if nonetheless the card balance becomes negative, the cardholder will or may be assessed a fee.[47]

TABLE 12: NEGATIVE BALANCE FEE FINDINGS

Scope of review	No negative balance fees		Negative balance fees		No fee info	
All agreements	**252**	**77.54%**	**31**	**9.54%**	**42**	**12.92%**
GPR cards	172	83.09%	25	12.08%	10	4.83%
Payroll cards	18	72.0%	3	12.0%	4	16.0%
Government benefit cards	37	56.92%	2	3.08%	26	40.00%
All other programs	25	89.29%	1	3.57%	2	7.14%
GPR only: 5 largest program managers by load volume	18	81.82%	4	18.18%	0	--
GPR only: 11 largest program managers by number of active cards	36	90.0%	4	10.0%	0	--

---

[46] *See* Attachment A at column X. Each agreement was designated as either Y (Yes), N (No), or No fee info (for agreements did not explicitly state that fees were not charged for negative balances and where Bureau staff was unable to locate any fee information generally for the program). For agreements designated Y, the specific type of fee and amount (where stated) are also listed in column X.

[47] Some agreements also state that repeated attempts to spend beyond the card balance will or may result in the prepaid account being closed. Bureau staff has doubts about whether or to what extent such charges are actually currently being assessed, as staff does not believe that there are many situations where such accounts could go negative. Staff also believes that, in practice, some of these programs may not charge such fees even though the fees are included in their account agreements.

For those agreements noting that negative balance or similar fees might be charged (excluding those that offered a formal opt-in overdraft service), Bureau staff found that the fee amounts (where specifically listed in the account agreement) ranged from $5 to $29. Two agreements were identified as charging fees based on a specified annual percentage rate, and one charged a fee of $0.15 for every $1 of negative balance up to a maximum fee of $36.

3.5 FDIC or NCUSIF pass-through deposit or share insurance

Bureau staff examined prepaid account agreements for language, if any, addressing the applicability of FDIC or NCUSIF pass-through deposit or share insurance to the program. Agreements were divided into four categories: (1) those that state that the program was FDIC or NCUSIF-insured (including agreements that explain insurance coverage depends on card registration and/or that it only applies to funds held by a bank or credit union in a pooled account associated with the program); (2) those that imply that the program was FDIC or NCUSIF insured by stating that the issuer is an FDIC or NCUSIF-insured institution, but that do not address FDIC or NCUSIF insurance coverage for the program; (3) those that do not address FDIC or NCUSIF insurance at all; and (4) those that explicitly state that the program is not insured.[48]

Bureau staff has anecdotally observed that some GPR card providers disclose the existence of FDIC pass-through deposit insurance coverage or that the issuing bank is an FDIC-insured institution on their retail packaging, often quite prominently. This Study, however, did not examine pass-through insurance statements made on GPR cards' retail packaging. Likewise, the Study did not examine pass-through insurance statements made on prepaid programs' other marketing materials or on their websites.

---

[48] *See* Attachment A at column Y for the full text of each agreement's FDIC/NCUSIF insurance provisions. *See* columns Z through AC for Bureau staff's analysis of those provisions.

Table 13 summarizes Bureau staff's findings regarding FDIC or NCUSIF pass-through deposit or share insurance.

TABLE 13: FDIC OR NCUSIF PASS-THROUGH DEPOSIT OR SHARE INSURANCE FINDINGS

Scope of review	Insured		Insurance implied		Silent		Not insured	
All agreements	**214**	**65.85%**	**56**	**17.23%**	**20**	**6.15%**	**35**	**10.77%**
GPR cards	127	61.35%	40	19.32%	14	6.76%	26	12.56%
Payroll cards	16	64.0%	5	20.0%	1	4.0%	3	12.0%
Government benefit cards	64	98.46%	0	--	1	1.54%	0	--
All other programs	7	25.0%	11	39.29%	4	14.29%	6	21.43%
GPR only: 5 largest program managers by load volume	18	81.82%	3	13.64%	1	4.55%	0	--
GPR only: 11 largest program managers by number of active cards	29	72.50%	6	15.0%	1	2.50%	4	10.0%

3.6 General disclosure of fee information

Bureau staff noted whether each prepaid account agreement reviewed contains fee tables or other explanations of fees charged by the program. As noted above, where a prepaid account agreement does not include fee information, staff attempted to locate a separate document containing fee information for the program. Agreements were divided into two categories: (1) those that contain fee information for the program, and (2) those that appear to contain very limited or no fee information.[49] Table 14 summarizes staff's findings on general disclosure of fee information.

TABLE 14: GENERAL DISCLOSURE OF FEE INFORMATION FINDINGS

Scope of review	Contains fee information		Limited or no fee information	
All agreements	278	85.54%	47	14.46%
GPR cards	196	94.69%	11	5.31%
Payroll cards	19	76.0%	6	24.0%
Government benefit cards	38	58.46%	27	51.54%
All other programs	25	89.29%	3	10.71%
GPR only: 5 largest program managers by load volume	22	100%	0	--
GPR only: 11 largest program managers by number of active cards	44	100%	0	--

[49] *See* Attachment A at column AD for the full text of each agreement's fee information. *See* columns AE and AF for Bureau staff's analysis of those provisions. For the text included in column AD, Bureau staff included fee information from fee charts or other lists of fees in the account agreements. As noted above, where a prepaid account agreement did not include fee information, staff searched for a separate document containing fee information. Staff also included the text of additional paragraphs regarding ATM fees, international transaction fees, and similar provisions where those provisions followed the primary discussion of fees. Staff did not attempt to locate such provisions elsewhere throughout the agreements.